KIM K. SANDERS

CONFESSIONS FROM THE THIRD REALM

Words That Activate The Heavens,
Pierce The Forces of Darkness, and Shift Atmospheres

Unless otherwise indicated, all scripture quotations are taken from the Kings James Version of the Bible.

CONFESSIONS FROM THE THIRD REALM

Words That Activate The Heavens, Pierce The Forces of Darkness and Shift Atmospheres

ISBN: 978-0-9966222-2-6

Copyright © 2017 Kim K. Sanders

Published by:

Kim K. Sanders International, LLC
P.O. Box 236
Little Rock, AR 72203
www.kimksanders.com

All rights reserved.

Printed in the United States of America.

This material is protected by the United States copyright laws. It is not to be copied or duplicated in whole or in part by any method without the written consent of the publisher.

CONTENTS

INTRODUCTION 1

BREAKING SOUL TIES 12

HELP ME LORD 14

THE GOD OF ABUNDANCE 16

HEALING CONFESSION 17

I'M HEALTHY 20

KIM'S DAILY CONFESSION 22

MY CHILDREN 30

LOVE AND THE BLOOD 33

MY HUSBAND 35

PEACE CONFESSION 40

I AM HAPPY 43

THE PRAYER OF RELEASE 45

FAVOR 47

I AM RELEASED INTO THE WORLD 51

WARFARE CONFESSION	56
WEALTH CONFESSION	58
LOOSE YOUR MONEY CONFESSION	61
PROSPERITY CONFESSION	65
I'M STRONG	68
THE BLESSING	71
ABOUT THE AUTHOR	73

INTRODUCTION

Words carry power; therefore, choose and use them wisely. The Word of God declares in Proverbs 18:21 *Death and life are in the power of the tongue: and they that love it shall eat the fruit thereof,* which means you have the ability to frame your world and life with your words, just like God framed this World with His words.

When you speak God's Word into the atmosphere, those words are filled with life substance. They have enough power within itself to come into manifestation.

As you speak and send the Word of God back to the third realm, those words must submit to and obey their Master. This is what it means when God says, His Word will not <u>come back</u> void but it will <u>accomplish</u> what it has been sent out to do.

So shall my word be that goeth forth out of my mouth: it shall not return unto me void, but it shall accomplish that which I please, and it shall prosper in the thing whereto I sent it. Isaiah 55:11

When the Word is sent back to the Heavens, angels harken to the voice of the Word and God fulfills the promise of those words.

Bless the Lord, ye his angels, that excel in strength, that do his commandments, hearkening unto the voice of his word. Psalm 103:20

God has to bring His Word to pass because God and the Word are one. And we know He cannot lie, neither can His Word.

The enemy understands the protocol of Heaven; this is the reason why he works overtime to deceive people by making them think that the Word of God does not work or that it does not take all of that. But the reality is, God watches over His Word to perform it. Hallelujah!

Then said the Lord unto me, Thou hast well seen: for I will hasten my word to perform it. Jeremiah 1:12

Words are the very things that activate the Heavens and penetrate the forces of darkness. Your words have the ability to shift situations, things and atmospheres in the earth.

The words written in this book are not just merely confessions, but rather prophetic words that all of Heaven recognize. These words are prophetic confessions that:

- make demons obey;
- release angels to harken to your voice; and
- are backed up by God because words belong to Him.

God created words and used them to create and form the Earth in Genesis chapter one. Because we are made in the image and likeness of who God is, we are made to imitate our Father.

And God said, Let us make man in our image, after our likeness: and let them have dominion over the fish of the sea, and over the fowl of the air, and over the cattle, and over all the earth, and over every creeping thing that creepeth upon the earth.

So God created man in his own image, in the image of God created he him; male and female created he them.

And God blessed them, and God said unto them, Be fruitful, and multiply, and replenish the earth, and subdue it: and have dominion over the fish of the sea, and over the fowl of the air, and over every living thing that moveth upon the earth. Genesis 1:26-28

God has given us the same authority to rule and reign in the earth. It's no different than when God told Adam to be fruitful and multiply and replenish the earth and subdue it and have dominion.

And God blessed them, and God said unto them, Be fruitful, and multiply, and replenish the earth, and subdue it: and have dominion over the fish of the sea, and over the fowl of the air, and over every living thing that moveth upon the earth.

The word dominion means the power or right of governing and controlling; sovereign authority. It also means to rule.

God gave Adam and mankind the dominion to rule in and govern the earth. God even gave Adam the authority to speak and name the animals.

And out of the ground the Lord God formed every beast of the field, and every fowl of the air; and brought them unto Adam to see what he would call them: and whatsoever Adam called every living creature, that was the name thereof. Genesis 2:19

If God gave Adam the right to name the animals, that means when Adam spoke to the animals they obeyed his words and command. It also proves that things obey and submit to the authority of words. Why, because it is legal in the spirit realm.

When Adams spoke in Genesis 2:23, *"This is now bone of my bones, and flesh of my flesh: she shall be called Woman, because she was taken out of Man,"* it was so. In other words, it was established and settled in the earth, therefore it became legislated and legitimate in Heaven.

The Authority of Jesus

Jesus was a man of authority and other people recognized the authority within him. When Jesus spoke, things obeyed him. One example was when Jesus spoke to the fig tree.

And on the morrow, when they were come from Bethany, he was hungry:

And seeing a fig tree afar off having leaves, he came, if haply he might find any thing thereon: and when he came to it, he found nothing but leaves; for the time of figs was not yet.

And Jesus answered and said unto it, No man eat fruit of thee hereafter for ever. And his disciples heard it. Mark 11:12-14

In Mark 11: 20-21 we see the manifestation of the fig tree obeying Jesus' words.

And in the morning, as they passed by, they saw the fig tree dried up from the roots.

And Peter calling to remembrance saith unto him, Master, behold, the fig tree which thou cursedst is withered away.

All throughout the four gospels we see that sickness, disease and demons obeyed Jesus when he spoke. Jesus rebuked demons with the Word of God.

What many people fail to realize is demons only recognize, respond and submit to the voice of the Word of God when spoken with authority, end of story. You can scream and yell all day long, but if you are void of the Word of God and power, demons will not obey your command. The only way to have full confidence that the Word of God will work on your behalf, is knowing the Word and being completely submitted to the Father. Your authority as a Believer comes from being filled with the Word of God in your heart and becoming one with the Father.

Not only was Jesus a man of authority, but He was a man under authority and full of the Word. Jesus was completely obedient and submitted to the will of His Father. He was one with God and the Word, therefore all of Heaven backed Jesus with power when He spoke the Word and His words were filled with authority.

The Word of God cannot work for you when you speak it, if you lack the Word and are disobedient to it. You have no power or authority when you are not subject to the very thing you need to rebuke the devil. Demons won't obey your voice or submit to you, because they know there's no authentic Word, obedience or authority in you. How can you use the Word of God against the enemy or expect for the Word to work on your behalf when you speak it, if you don't know or obey it? You can't! Angels won't even harken to the voice of your words.

Disobedience is not just sin, but disobedience is also when you hear God speaking, you know what His Word says, but yet you openly resist and reject His instructions. This my friend is called open rebellion and the bible says that open rebellion is the same as witchcraft.

For rebellion is as the sin of witchcraft, and stubbornness is as iniquity and idolatry. Because thou hast rejected the word of the Lord, he hath also rejected thee from being king. 1 Samuel 15:23

When you choose to disobey God and His Word, you are making a conscious, intelligent decision to rebel, "knowing" that God has spoken to you. It reveals that you don't reverence God or respect the most powerful weapon that He has given you to defeat your adversary.

Abiding In The Word

As I previously stated, Jesus was one with the Father and one with the Word, which indicates the Word of God was abiding in Him.

The word abide means to dwell, remain, continue, stay; to have one's abode, reside in, to submit or rest; expect.

The only way the Word of God can have life and authority when you speak it, is when it truly abides within your heart.

My son, attend to my words; incline thine ear unto my sayings.

Let them not depart from thine eyes; keep them in the midst of thine heart.

For they are life unto those that find them, and health to all their flesh. Keep thy heart with all diligence; for out of it are the issues of life. Proverbs 4:20-23

It is only when the Word of God abides, dwells and rests in you that you become one with the Father.

Abide in me, and I in you. As the branch cannot bear fruit of itself, except it abide in the vine; no more can ye, except ye abide in me.

I am the vine, ye are the branches: He that abideth in me, and I in him, the same bringeth forth much fruit: for without me ye can do nothing. John 15:4-5

The moment you decide to obey God's Word, you invite and make room for authority in your life to rule and reign. Once you become one with the Father and the Word, authority comes to live within you, because the Word of God births authentic authority. Now, authority and the Word has a resting place in your heart. The Word is no longer competing with disobedience and can produce fruit.

Now that authority is ruling and reigning within you, you have the ability to defeat the enemy, shift atmospheres, speak God's Word and it will come into divine manifestation. Why? Because the ground of your heart is now conducive for growth, multiplication and producing a harvest.

If ye abide in me, and my words abide in you, ye shall ask what ye will, and it shall be done unto you. John 15:7

One of the definitions of the word abide is to "expect."

When you abide in the Word and the Word abides in you, you can expect God's Word to come to pass when you speak it, because you are submitted to the Word and now the Word will submit to your command.

BREAKING SOUL TIES

In the Name of Jesus, I decree and declare as a Prophet of God that every soul-tie be severed and permanently broken from your past and that you are cleansed by the blood of Jesus and that you have no defilement from demonic attachments, demonic activations or demonic residue. I declare that the yoke of bondage has been broken from this very moment, in the Name of Jesus. I speak liberty over your soul, I decree that all aspects of your soul will be released from spiritual hindrances. I declare that all soul ties initiated by sexual intercourse, reinforced by emotional and mental bondage activated by the movement of demons through generational lineage are permanently broken by the power of God and in Jesus' name; I speak healing over any emotional, mental, physical or spiritual affliction to you!

I decree in Jesus' name that you are totally whole by the blood of Jesus! Now I come against any diabolical assignments or relationships that try to attach themselves to you and I declare that any satanic ungodly alliance that tries to attach themselves to you be destroyed. I pray the hand of God be stretched out against them, as they come in contact with the blood of Jesus and wrath of God. I release a blood shield around you and I declare that the anointing, fire walls, smoke screens and bloodline form a hedge of protection around you and hide you from the scourge of the enemy, making it impossible for them to trace you in the realm of the spirit and there shall be no perforations or penetrations to these hedges of protection, in Jesus' name, Amen!

HELP ME LORD

Help me Holy Spirit to be all that I can be today. I depend on you this day Holy Spirit to be my helper and my guide. I can do all things through Christ who strengthens me, because greater is He that is in me than he that is in the world; therefore I will walk in the spirit and not fulfill the lust of my flesh. [John 16:13, Philippians 4:13, 1John 4:4, Galatians 5:16]

I put a guard over my mouth and no corrupt communication will come out of my mouth. I will be quick to hear and slow to speak. I will hear counsel and receive instruction, that I may be wise in my latter end. [Ephesians 4:29, James 1:19, Proverbs19:20]

I will obey those who are in authority over me and walk in obedience to my parents for it is pleasing to the Lord. I walk in obedience to the Word of God. [Hebrews 13:17, Colossians, 3:20, Joshua 1:8]

I declare that I will not yield to temptation, but submit myself to God and resist the devil. I know the voice of the Holy Spirit and I obey His leading. [Matthew 26:41, James 4:7, John 10:27]

Father, I decree that the words of my mouth and the meditation of my heart be acceptable in thy sight O Lord, my strength and my redeemer. [Psalms 19:14]

THE GOD OF ABUNDANCE

You are the God of abundance and no lack; therefore, I remind You of my blood covenant. I have a blood covenant with You Father, because of the blood shed of Jesus the Christ. I have been redeemed for the curse of the law according to Galatians 3: 13-14, which gives me access to all the promises from Your Word.

I am a tither and a giver, which qualifies me and positions me for You to rebuke the devourer for my sake according to Malachi 3:10-11. Now in the name of Jesus, I declare that the windows of Heaven are opened to me to pour out a blessing that there will not be room enough to receive all the blessings You have for me.

It is You Father that gives me the power and ability to get wealth, therefore I decree and declare that I am anointed to prosper. I declare that wealth and riches are in my house and every promise from Your Word is yes and amen, in Jesus' name.

HEALING CONFESSION

I refuse, reject and resist sickness, disease and the spirit of infirmity. I disallow and disagree with sickness and disease. I forbid sickness and disease. I deny and disown you. I say no to you. I repel and deny you. You have no power over me; therefore, I renounce you in the name of Jesus. Spirit of infirmity, I bind you in the name of Jesus and I now command you to disappear. I speak to you and say that you will not manifest yourself in me. You will not have your way, therefore I bind you and all of your fruits. You will not rule because Jesus is Lord over my life and body. Because I'm in covenant with God, I have a right to receive my healing, by and through the blood that was shed for me.

I see and announce that the blood of Jesus is against you satan; therefore, absolutely nothing can penetrate or come against the blood of Jesus. So I plead the blood of Jesus over my body right now and I decree and declare that the blood has healed my body. I stand fully clothed in my righteousness as a Son/Daughter and I receive my healing NOW, in Jesus' name and I declare the name

Jehovah Rophe. I worship that Name, I adore the name Jehovah Rophe as my Healer and I thank you Father in Jesus' name.

Now I thank you Lord that healing overtakes me, healing saturates me, healing dominates me, healing possesses me, healing empowers me, healing engulfs me, healing overpowers me, healing surrounds me, healing penetrates me, healing overrides in me, healing fills me, healing abides in me, healing lives in me, healing remains in me, healing dwells in me and healing manifests itself in me; it's visible in me. I wear healing as my garment, healing clothes me, it hugs me. Healing loves me, it's like a magnet, it sticks to me, gravitates to me. I embrace healing. I drink healing, I eat healing and I breathe healing.

Healing is my portion; it is my promise, it's my daily bread. Healing is in my DNA, healing runs through my blood stream, it's in my veins. Healing invades my body, healing is in my joints, it's in my bones, in my tissues. Healing is in my mind, in my brain, in my emotions; healing resides in my soul.

Healing floods my body. Healing is raining on the inside of me. Healing stands strong in me, it covers me from head to toe. I'm infected with the healing virus. I take a shot of healing. Healing is my prescription. Healing is my drug, I receive it every day. I overdose on healing. Healing is overflowing and running over in my body. Healing is like a best friend, I call it every day.

Healing circulates in me, it washes me clean of anything unclean. Healing consumes me, healing overwhelms me, healing bombards my body, it raids my body. I digest healing. Healing is pouring in me continuously, it never stops; it's always flowing, it's unending, it's infinite, it's always present, forever reigning in me, everlasting. Healing rests in me, it remains in me forever and ever, in Jesus' name, Amen!

I'M HEALTHY

In the name of Jesus, I decree and declare my body functions in the way God created it to function. I take care of my body because my body is the temple of God. I decree that I have the grace and anointing of God to eat right. I despise junk food and I eliminate all food that's not good for my body. I desire healthy foods that are good for my body and I feed my body life. I only eat food that causes my body to thrive; therefore, I only deposit life food into my body and my body operates at its full capacity.

I am anointed and graced by God to exercise. I embrace exercise because it does my body good. I love exercising because it makes me feel good inside. When I exercise, I reap the benefits of mental clarity and good rest. Exercising enables me to have a strong heart and lots of energy. My joints are flexible and I move about with these.

I make myself drink plenty of water and I get plenty of sleep. God gives me sweet and uninterrupted sleep every night. I take the necessary vitamins and nutrients that my body needs daily. I walk in Divine health and Divine Healing, therefore, no sickness or disease can touch my body in Jesus' name. I declare I am in good and perfect health in Jesus' name, Amen.

KIM'S DAILY CONFESSION

I am the redeemed of the Lord and whatever I say is so, therefore, I am anointed to pray to get results. I am the righteousness of God in Christ Jesus, created in His workmanship. I am firmly established in the Word of God, studying to show myself approved unto God, not being ashamed so that I rightly divide the Word of truth. I am the head and not the tail. I am above only and not beneath.

Jesus made unto me wisdom, righteousness, sanctification, redemption, peace, joy, healing, deliverance and prosperity because I have been redeemed from the curse of the law; therefore, I have a right to my inheritance, as a seed of Abraham.

I decree in Jesus' name that I will never be broke another day in my life! Let the Lord be magnified, which has pleasure in the prosperity of Kim (say your name here), therefore, I am anointed to prosper. I declare that whatever I put my hands to, it shall prosper. God gives me the power to get wealth; therefore ideas, concepts and insight from the Holy Ghost come to me daily to produce big money for the kingdom of God. I am a money magnet, therefore, money is drawn to me. Money comes to me now! I call money from the east, south, north and west. Money obeys me. I declare that I am a multi-millionaire for the glory of God.

I say that I am the lender and not the borrower, so I decree that the wealth of the wicked is transferred to me now! I say that unexpected income comes into my hands, my ministry, my business and my household. Men give into my bosom, good measure, pressed down, shaken together, running over, for with the same measure that I give it is measured back to me. I am a blessed woman of God and money hunts me down. Blessings come on me and overtake me. I'm blessed in the city and blessed in the field. I'm blessed coming in and blessed going out. Everywhere I go, I am blessed. I'm blessed with all spiritual blessings in heavenly places in Christ Jesus. Wealth and riches are in my house, ministry and business. Goodness and mercy follow after me all the days of my life.

In Jesus' name I decree that I will never be sick another day in my life. I forbid any sickness and disease to come upon my body. I decree that every organ and every tissue of my body functions in the perfection to which God created it to function and I forbid any malfunction in this body, in the name of Jesus. Jesus was wounded for my transgressions and was bruised for my iniquities; the chastisement of my peace was upon Him, therefore by His stripes I am healed and made whole. My family and I are immune to all sickness and disease; they have no place in our life. Every germ, virus and infection that touches my body instantly dies.

I decree in Jesus' name that I will never be depressed another day in my life. The peace of God rules in my heart because I trust in the Lord with all my heart and I lean not unto my own understanding, but in all my ways I acknowledge Him and He directs my path. I wear the garment of praise for the spirit of heaviness; therefore, I will bless the Lord at all times and His praise shall continually be in my mouth. I am far from oppression for I do not fear; and from terror for it shall not come near me. God has not given me the spirit of fear, but I have power, love and a sound mind. I also have the mind of Christ and my mind is being renewed by the Word of God daily.

I have an anointing from the Holy One and I know all things, therefore, I have ears to hear what the Spirit of the Lord is saying, to me in all situations. Through wisdom I build my house and by understanding, it is established. I have the spirit of wisdom, revelation and knowledge in all things and the wisdom of God is formed within me. As I speak God's Words of wisdom, I bring peace and victory to my life. I will not walk in darkness today, for the Holy Spirit will guide me into all truth. Satan cannot overcome me, for God has given me a mouth and wisdom the enemy cannot gainsay nor resist.

My family and I are delivered from the powers of darkness and translated into the kingdom of God's dear son. No evil shall come near me and my family because we dwell in the secret place of the Most High God and abide under the shadow of the Almighty. The blood of Jesus covers us everywhere that we go. The blood of Jesus protects us from all harm, danger, evil, accidents, car accidents, freak accidents, tragedy and death. Long life satisfies me and my household. I decree and declare that angels are encamped around and about us, taking charge over us, keeping us in all our ways.

I overcome all the fiery darts of the enemy and nothing can harm me because greater is He that is in me than he that is in the world. I wear the whole armor of God and I resist the wiles of the devil. I have all power over the enemy, therefore, I bind all principalities, powers and the rulers of darkness of this world. I break every power of the enemy and cancel every assignment against me, my household, my family, those assigned to me, my ministry, our finances and our health, and I loose total life prosperity in the name of Jesus.

I am filled with the knowledge of the Lord's will in all wisdom and spiritual understanding. My footsteps today are ordered of God. I will not walk in the counsel of the ungodly, nor sit in the way of sinners. My delight is in the law of the Lord and in His law I meditate day and night. This book of the law will not depart out of my mouth because I meditate on it day and night that I may observe to do all that's written so that I can make my way prosperous and have good success. Because I delight myself in the Lord, He will give me the desires of my heart.

I am like a tree planted by the rivers of water that bringeth forth His fruit in His season. I am anointed to remove burdens and destroy yokes. I bring the deliverance power of God with me everywhere I go. When people look at me, they see Jesus and the glory of God. I stick out wherever I go because I am a light that cannot be hid and people are drawn to Jesus because of the anointing that's within me. The love of God flows through me and into the lives of others because I have the compassion of Jesus. I am blessed to be a blessing and I always have more than enough to give into the lives of others and into the kingdom of God. I deposit the joy of the Lord into the lives of others because the joy of the Lord is my strength. Every day I have joy because I speak words that bring life to me and others. No corrupt communication shall come out of my mouth today but that which is good to the edifying that it may minister grace to the hearers. For I speak anointed words of faith and edification filled with power.

I shall not die, but live and declare the works of the Lord. I minister the Word of God all over this world and my gifts make room for me and bring me before great men. I am a mouthpiece, therefore, I speak the oracles of God and bring deliverance to multitudes. I decree that when I minister, demons are cast out, broken hearts are mended, the sick are healed, blind eyes see and deaf ears hear. The peace, the joy and the worship of the Father shall be released, and the glory of God will always appear and the captives set free because I am a glory carrier. I decree and declare that signs and wonders follow every time that I minister to God's people and lives are changed all over this world.

Doors are constantly being opened for me to minister to God's people all over this World. People are using their ability and influence to open doors for me daily. My face and name appear before pastors, bishops and leaders all over this world that need the ministry gift that's in me. In Jesus' name I depend upon the Holy Spirit to make the connections and do the work. I am God's yielded vessel to be used however He chooses.

I love the Lord with my whole heart and have a passion for the Word of God. I will not let the Word of God depart from before my eyes, for it is life to me. I have found it and it is health and healing to all my flesh. I am led everyday by the Spirit of the Lord and not by my feelings or emotions. I walk in the spirit and I do not fulfill the lust of my flesh. My flesh is in subjection to my spirit. I declare that my spirit is the dominant one because I continue to feed it the Word of God. I'm only subject to the law of the spirit of life in Christ Jesus. I walk in the fruit of the spirit and the gifts of the spirit are manifest through me mightily. The Lord will perfect that which concerneth me. I am anointed to fulfill my definite divine purpose and the will of God for my life, in Jesus' name, it is so.

MY CHILDREN

I decree and declare that my children are smart, intelligent and excel in all that they do in life. Great is the peace of my children. My children are anointed of God. The Bible declares in Proverbs 11:21 the seed of the righteous shall be delivered, therefore, I declare that my children are delivered from the powers of darkness and translated into the kingdom of the Lord Jesus Christ.

I declare that my children are prosperous in every area of their lives and flourish in all that they do. My children are completely healthy, happy and whole with nothing broken and nothing missing in their lives. I declare that my children love and serve God with their whole heart. I decree and declare they hunger and thirst for righteousness. I decree that my children are saved, sanctified and filled with the Holy Ghost.

I decree and declare that my children are covered by the blood of Jesus everywhere they go today, from the top of their heads to the soles of their feet. I draw a blood line around my children. I decree and declare the blood of Jesus surrounds them. I decree that everywhere their feet tread, the blood of Jesus goes before them right now, in the name of Jesus. I declare that the blood protects them from all harm, danger, evil, accidents, car accidents, freak accidents, tragedy and death. Long life satisfies my children. No weapon formed against my children shall prosper and every tongue that rises against them in judgment, I condemn in the name of Jesus. I decree and declare angels are encamped around and about my children. They take charge over them and keep them in all of their ways.

I decree and declare that my children fulfill their God-given assignment; therefore, the eyes of their understanding are enlightened concerning their definite divine purpose. My children walk in divine wisdom and godly counsel. My children walk in the spirit daily and do not fulfill the lust of their flesh. My children are free from sin, drugs, alcohol, any type of bondage and all things contrary to the things of God. I decree that my children are doers of the Word of God and I declare they know His voice. My children are obedient and they fear God. I declare that my children have a sound mind and make intelligent, fruitful, sober decisions in all of their endeavors.

I love my children and I declare that my children love me. My children have integrity and their name is associated with riches, wealth and prosperity, in the name of Jesus. My children are mighty upon this earth and I declare that there is nothing impossible with God for my children. They can do all things through Christ who strengthens them. In Jesus' name, I declare my children are blessed.

LOVE AND THE BLOOD

Absolutely nothing can uproot me because I'm deeply planted in the Word of the Most High God. Love is deeply planted within me. My seeds are love, joy, peace, brokenness, compassion and strength. I water my seeds daily. My seeds grow daily and produce life.

Love flows through me like a river, washing away all hurt, disappointments and offenses. I wear love and compassion as my garments. I'm clothed in God's love. God is love, therefore, I am love because I'm made in His image and in His likeness. I wear love daily, it's in my DNA; it's who I am. I am love and love is me. When I look in the mirror I see love. When people look at me they see love all over me because it permeates from the inside out.

I eat love, I drink love, I breathe love. Love runs through my veins like a blood transfusion because of the blood of Jesus. The blood of Jesus cleanses and washes me. I receive my blood transfusion right now, in the name of Jesus. Because His blood delivers me, I deliver others through the name and blood of Jesus. Because of the blood I'm whole with nothing broken and nothing missing in my life.

Because of the blood, I'm righteous. The blood of Jesus covers me. Absolutely nothing can come against the blood of Jesus, therefore, it saturates me; it penetrates my spirit, soul and body. It invades my mind and protects me from the powers of the enemy. Absolutely no one can come against the blood of Jesus; therefore, I say that the blood of Jesus is against you satan in the name of Jesus. I appropriate the blood over my life, my household, my family and those attached to me in the name of Jesus. I decree and declare that the blood protects us from all harm, danger, evil, accidents, freak accidents, car accidents, tragedy and death in Jesus' name. Long life satisfies me and mine, in Jesus' name.

MY HUSBAND

I am a virtuous woman that ministers life to my husband's every need. I do him good and not evil all the days of my life. Because of me, he obtains favor of the Lord. The fire of God falls in our marriage daily. I'm anointed to serve him in every area and I'm sensitive to his needs. I submit to my own husband and the heart of my husband safely trusts in me and he has no need of spoil. Besides me there is no other. I rock his world. My breasts satisfy him at all times all the days of his life and everything that he has need of is all in me.

He drinks from my fountain only and he's completely satisfied. I'm a crown and joy to him and he calls me blessed. I have creative abilities to be the best wife in the world. We communicate effectively daily and we're always on one accord. I'm always in tune with the Holy Spirit concerning my husband. I have crystal clear hearing from the Holy Spirit because I know God's voice and a voice of a stranger I do not follow.

I break the powers of the enemy that try to come against my husband and I decree in the name of Jesus that every assignment and every attack sent out against him from the enemy and the forces of darkness is canceled by the blood of the Lamb. No weapon formed against him shall prosper and every tongue that rises against him in judgment he condemns, for this is his heritage as a servant of God. I plead the blood of Jesus over him everywhere he goes. He wears the whole armor of God and is able to stand against the wiles of the devil, because he studies to show himself approved unto God, not being ashamed so that he rightly divides the word of truth.

My husband is the priest and prophet of our home. The word of God is his inspiration and he seeks God daily. My husband is quick to obey the leading of the Holy Spirit. Sin, lack, insufficiency, debt, sickness and disease have no place in his life because he is redeemed from the curse of the law.

He has ears to hear what the Spirit of the Lord is saying to him, therefore, he knows God's voice and the voice of a stranger he will not follow. The eyes of his understanding are being enlightened concerning his purpose. My husband has the sensitivity of the Holy

Spirit and ministers to the needs of his family. He loves me as Christ loved the church and gives himself to his family as Christ gave himself to the Church. The love of God is in him and flows through him into the lives of his family and others. The love, peace and joy of the Lord are released into his heart.

I bind the spirit of carnality and take authority over carnal thinking and release the things of the spirit directly to his spirit man, which will minister to and penetrate his soul. I decree that the blood of Jesus covers his mind, and his thoughts will line up with the Word of God because he has the mind of Christ. His mind is transformed and renewed by the Word of God daily.

I bind the spirit of fear from his life for God has not given him a spirit of fear but he has power, love and a sound mind. My husband has the spirit of wisdom and revelation in the knowledge of God. He is a doer of God's Word. He walks in the spirit, therefore, he will not fulfill the lust of his flesh. He walks in the fruit of the spirit and it is manifest in his life.

His delight is in the law of the Lord and in God's law he meditates day and night, that he may observe to do all that's written, so he can make his way prosperous and cause good success to come to his family. He is firmly established in the Word and is like a tree, planted by the rivers of water that brings forth his fruit in his season. His leaf shall not wither and whatever he does shall prosper. My husband is a great provider and loves to give. He has favor with God and with man. He is anointed to prosper. My husband is blessed in the city and he's blessed in the field. He's blessed coming in and blessed going out. He is the head and not the tail, above only and not beneath. He is the lender and not the borrower. My husband walks in divine health and divine wealth. He walks in supernatural favor, increase and promotion.

My husband is all that the Word of God says he is. He always agrees with God and not with man, making confessions aloud. He receives godly counsel and has the wisdom of God formed within him. He uses wisdom when making decisions for his household and in business dealings. My husband is filled with the knowledge of the Lord's will in all wisdom and spiritual understanding.

He is known in the city gates and his gifts make room for him and bring him before great men. He is a man of righteousness and is known for his integrity. Multitudes come to Jesus because He is a city that is set upon a hill and His light cannot be hid. My husband is a godly example to his family and others around him. He ministers life to people everywhere he goes.

The joy of the Lord is my husband's strength and the peace of God rules in his heart, because he trusts in the Lord with his whole heart and leans not unto his own understanding, but he acknowledges the Lord in all his ways and God directs his path; therefore, his footsteps are ordered of the Lord.

He's the best husband in the world; he satisfies me and he applies Holy Ghost given creative ideas to enhance the romance in our marriage. My husband is anointed to fulfill my emotional and sexual needs.

He will fulfill the will of God for his life!

PEACE CONFESSION

Absolutely nothing overtakes me; absolutely nothing upsets me because I let the peace of God rule in my heart. I'm not caught off guard and taken by surprise by any bad reports or tragedies of any kind because God has not given me the spirit of fear but I have power, love and a sound mind. I have the mind of God; His grace is sufficient for me and His strength is perfect in my weakness.

I trust in the Lord with my whole heart and lean not unto my own understanding. In all my ways, I acknowledge Him as He directs my path. I dwell in the secret place of the most High God and I abide in the shadow of the Almighty. He is my refuge and my fortress; in Him I trust. I keep my mind stayed and fixed on Him. I let peace be my umpire. I meditate on God's Word day and night; it is my daily bread.

I do not worry about anything; therefore, I am stress and drama free. I mind my own business unless God makes it my business. I don't allow anything negative to enter my spirit or soul. I don't allow others to upset me, frustrate me or confuse me. I receive only life in my spirit, soul and body. I think on things that are pure, just, honest, true, lovely and of a good report, in the name of Jesus. My heart is filled with only life and there's no room for anything other than life and peace. I'm filled with the knowledge of the Lord's will in all wisdom and spiritual understanding and I decree and declare that I know what to do in every situation, which gives me peace.

Nothing other than life can penetrate my heart, my spirit, soul or body because I guard my heart with all diligence. I wear the whole armor of God and I forcefully resist the wiles of the devil. My mind, my thoughts and my soul are only subject to the Word of God and the spirit of life in Christ Jesus. I receive only life!

Peace stands still and strong in me; it saturates and penetrates my mind, my soul and my body from the top of my head to the souls of my feet. I feel peace all over me. I'm not moved by what I see, feel or hear but only by what God says. I embrace peace, I digest peace, I breathe peace, I inhale and exhale peace.

Peace abides, dwells and remains in my soul. I have peace in the midst of confusion and turmoil. Nothing can shake or break me because my soul is anchored in peace and I'm completely whole, with nothing broken or missing in my spirit, soul or body. I love peace and peace loves me. Peace overwhelms me; it overtakes me and it's strong in my heart and soul.

I speak peace into my atmosphere. I say peace be still! Peace abides in my home, in my marriage, in my husband, in my children and in every area of my life. When people come in contact with me, they come in contact with peace because I'm a carrier of the peace of God. God is peace and peace is in me now. I release and I deposit peace into the lives of others. I'm a peacemaker and I submit to the God of peace.

Peace rains on and in my home. When people come into my home, they feel the spirit of peace in the atmosphere. I release peace into every situation I face. Peace fills the atmosphere everywhere I go. Peace takes up residence in my spirit, soul and body. I feel peace right now; I say peace, peace, peace!

I AM HAPPY

I am happy. I am full of joy because the joy of the Lord is my strength.

I wear the garment of praise for the spirit of heaviness. I abide in the presence of God daily because in His presence is fullness of joy. I decree and declare that I have unspeakable joy every day. I laugh every day because laughter is good for my soul. A merry heart does good like medicine; therefore, I surround myself with positive happy people that encourage me, enhance me, make me laugh and make my life better.

I smile daily because I'm thankful and grateful. My smile is contagious and it affects everyone around me. I smile because I'm happy. I smile because I'm in my right mind. I smile because I'm healthy. Lord, I smile because I trust You. I smile because God takes care of my every need. I smile because I'm alive.

I'm thankful that I woke up this morning, which makes me happy. I'm happy because God loves me. I'm happy because God always protects me. I'm happy because God gives me the desires of my heart. I'm happy because I have the privilege of serving my God and others. I'm happy because I get to worship my Father. I sing because I'm happy and I wear the oil of gladness; thank you Lord that Joy fills my spirit, soul and body daily in the name of Jesus.

I think on those things that are true, honest, just, pure and lovely and I think on those things that are of a good report, which gives me peace and makes me happy. My happiness is not based on others. My happiness is not connected to what other people do or don't do for me, but my happiness is a choice. I choose to be happy. Fulfilling my definite divine purpose gives me joy and makes me happy. I have joy because Jesus shed his blood just for me, so I can be free to be happy.

THE PRAYER OF RELEASE

Father in the name of Jesus, I repent of holding on to every aspect of my past. I repent of and renounce all self-deceptions, delusions and counterfeit works, produced by my acceptance of false prophecies.

I renounce any point of acceptance of lies about me by satan and his allies. I intercept and destroy all lies from satan that were spoken to me by any persons who were associated with me during my infancy, childhood, adolescence or in my adulthood. I renounce any self-imposed curses or self-imposed bondage that would hinder my definite divine purpose, established by statements I have made or by my acceptance of statements spoken concerning me by parents, siblings, relatives, neighbors, friends, former friends, relationship partners, brethren in the church, co-workers or persons unknown to me.

I cast down all strongholds on my mind and my emotions concerning the activations produced by words spoken against me or spoken against the divine prophecies concerning my future, my well-being or my divine purpose. I renounce all hurt, disappointments and fear, which have produced secrecy, guilt, hidden shame, deception, hypocrisy and pretense in my life.

I decree the immediate destruction of every negative seed sown in my life; I sever the root of childhood abuse, childhood devastation, previous tragedies, moral deterioration, abandonment, grief, parental rejection, parental betrayal, spousal rejection and family betrayal and I decree that all of these roots will be chopped and permanently dissolved so that I may experience total liberty in Christ.

Now Lord, I dust myself off from the stress and mental torment of my past, and in the name of Jesus Christ, I command abundant liberty in my soul and mentality, causing me to focus and concentrate on that which is important to my destiny. I decree that the blood of Jesus is now applied to cleanse and heal every wound created by the words, actions and impressions of others concerning me. I decree that I am set free from the yoke of bondage and every sin that so easily beset me in the past. In Jesus' name I decree and declare that I am no longer a victim or possess the victim spirit and its mentality. Lord you said in John 8:36, *"If the Son shall make you free ye shall be free indeed."* Lord I thank you that I am free, in Jesus' name. Amen!

FAVOR

According to the Word of God, I expect the favor of God today in all of my endeavors and affairs. I decree and declare uncommon, extravagant, unlimited unexpected favor is released on my behalf. I declare that I have featured status and unlimited access.

I decree and declare that everywhere I go I have favor with God and with man that produces supernatural increase and promotion.

But the Lord was with Joseph, and shewed him mercy, and gave him favour in the sight of the keeper of the prison. Genesis 39:21

I decree I have favor that produces restoration of everything that the enemy has stolen from me.

And I will give this people favour in the sight of the Egyptians: and it shall come to pass, that, when ye go, ye shall not go empty. Exodus 3:21

I decree and declare I have favor that produces honor in the midst of my adversaries.

And the Lord gave the people favour in the sight of the Egyptians. Moreover the man Moses was very great in the land of Egypt, in the sight of Pharaoh's servants, and in the sight of the people. Exodus 11:3

I declare I have favor that produces increased assets, especially in the area of real estate.

And of Naphtali he said, O Naphtali, satisfied with favour, and full with the blessing of the Lord: possess thou the west and the south. Deuteronomy 33:23

God I thank you that I have favor that produces great victories in the midst of great impossibilities.

For it was of the Lord to harden their hearts, that they should come against Israel in battle, that he might destroy them utterly, and that they might have no favour, but that he might destroy them, as the Lord commanded Moses. Joshua 11:20

I decree and declare I have favor that produces recognition even when i seem the least likely to receive it.

And Saul sent to Jesse, saying, Let David, I pray thee, stand before me; for he hath found favour in my sight. 1 Samuel 16:22.

I say that I have favor that produces prominence and preferential treatment.

And the king loved Esther above all the women, and she obtained grace and favour in his sight more than all the virgins; so that he set the royal crown upon her head, and made her queen instead of Vashti. Esther 2:17

I declare that I walk in favor that produces petitions granted even by ungodly civil authorities and I have favor that causes policies, rules, regulations and laws to be changed and reversed to my advantage.

If I have found favour in the sight of the king, and if it pleases the king to grant my petition, and to perform my request, let the king and Haman come to the banquet that I shall prepare for them, and I will do tomorrow as the king hath said. Esther 8:5.

Thank you Lord that I have favor that produces battles won that I don't have to fight because you Lord will fight them for me.

For they got not the land in possession by their own sword, neither did their own arm save them: but thy right hand, and thine arm, and the light of thy countenance, because thou hadst a favour unto them. Psalm 44:3.

I AM RELEASED INTO THE WORLD

Thank you Lord that doors of utterance and opportunities are opened to me all around the world. I decree and declare that covenant connections are being made and released to me right now. I declare that people are using their influence, favor, ability and power on my behalf in the name of Jesus.

My gifts make room for me and bring me before great men all over this world. I decree and declare that I am in High demand and Leaders all over this world are calling me. My name, my face, my website and my messages appear before Leaders, Pastors, Bishops, Apostles, Prophets, Celebrities, Producers, Political Leaders, Colleges, Organizations, Businesses, Companies and High-Profiles all over this world. They have need of the gifts within me. I grace T.V. shows, T.V. stations, radio stations, platforms, stages, auditoriums and stadiums all over this world. I receive invitations daily by phone, via emails and in person, in Jesus' name.

God has not given me the spirit of fear, but I have power, love and a sound mind. Perfect love casts out all fear and I decree and declare that I have perfect love manifesting in me daily and the bowels of my compassion are opened up wide for God's people in the name of Jesus.

I declare in Jesus' name that I am anointed to destroy the powers of darkness off of the minds of God's people, minister deliverance and set the captives free. I decree and declare that I am anointed to loose the bands of wickedness, undo the heavy burdens, to let the oppressed go free and break every yoke that I come in contact with according to Isaiah 58:6, because the Life of God abides in me. I have God's power and Word dwelling on the inside of me and I release it everywhere I go. I decree that when people come in contact with me, they come in contact with God because I carry His presence on the inside of me.

I declare that I am anointed to awaken the spirit, change the soul and enhance the body through healing. I am anointed to stimulate, educate and motivate people all over this world to activate Life. I decree and declare that lives are changed, by the power of God all over this world everywhere I go. I decree and declare that I travel the four corners of the world; the East, the South, the North and the West in Jesus' name. I confess that I go to Nations and Nations come to me, in the name of Jesus. I decree and declare that as I go into Cities, States and Countries, the strongman of that City must be subject to me by the blood and name of Jesus Christ; therefore, I bind the strong man of every City, State and Country that my feet will tread upon and I take authority over them in Jesus' name.

I decree and declare that greater is He that is in me, than he that is in the world, therefore I have the victory everywhere I go in Jesus' name. I know and understand my authority as a son/daughter of God and I announce that I am known all over this world as the Doctor of Deliverance, ordained by God. I decree and declare in the name of Jesus, that ABSOLUTELY NO demon will be able to stand in my presence and must bow at the name of Jesus. I declare that demons are uncomfortable in my presence by the power of God and through the blood of Jesus I declare they fear my presence, because I carry the same presence that raised Jesus from the dead. Demons tremble in my presence at the mention of the name and blood of Jesus. I decree and declare that when I come on the scene I bring the resurrected power of the blood of Jesus on the scene to cast out every demon in the atmosphere. I decree and declare that Jesus has given me power to tread upon serpents and scorpions and power over the enemy and nothing shall by any means hurt me; therefore, demons are subject to my voice, command and authority and they come out immediately, by the name and blood of Jesus.

I decree and declare that healings are manifest and demons are cast out when I pray, speak, preach, dance, sing, play and release prophetic sounds from the third realm. I decree and declare that I am a power shifter; therefore, I declare that as I come on the scene and walk into a room, atmospheres change and shift because I'm a carrier of the glory of God in the name of Jesus. I decree and declare that I cast out unclean spirits, deaf and dumb spirits and I cast out all that are possessed of devils.

I decree and declare that as I lay hands on the sick, all manner of sickness and all that are diseased are healed by the name and blood of Jesus. I declare that the sick recover and are made completely whole by the blood of

Jesus with signs and wonders following. I decree and declare the gifts of the spirit are manifest everywhere I go in the name of Jesus. I decree that miracles are manifest everywhere I go, blind eyes are opened, deaf ears hear and the dumb speak in Jesus' name. I decree and declare the Luke 4:18 anointing operates in my life, in Jesus' name Amen!

The Spirit of the Lord is upon me, because he hath anointed me to preach the gospel to the poor; he hath sent me to heal the brokenhearted, to preach deliverance to the captives, and recovering of sight to the blind, to set at liberty them that are bruised. Luke 4:18

WARFARE CONFESSION

As I stand in the authority and stand clothed in the mantle of the Lord Jesus Christ, my prayers are like arrows. I target and annihilate the hidden agenda of the enemy and I hit bulls-eye in the realm of the Spirit every time I pray. I hit every fiery dart, tactic and scheme of the enemy with the Word, the blood and name of Jesus, by the power of the Most High God.

I shine the light of God's Word on every dark place the enemy hides and I uncover strategies, covert operations and render them null and void. I arrest interferences, every demonic influence and I cancel, abort, nullify and dismantle all plans, plots and ploys against me, my household, my ministry, my finances and those assigned and connected to me.

I decree and declare that there will be no more negotiations, spiritual abortions or miscarriages and I overthrow setbacks, sabotages and disappointments in the name of Jesus. I obliterate satanic wombs, satanic incubations and every diabolical assignment designed to hinder, distract, frustrate, paralyze, block, delay, suppress or prevent the grace and will of God for my life, my family and those connected and assigned to me.

I prohibit and disallow satanic databases, satanic manifestations or satanic harassments and I forcefully resist all deceptions, lies and confusion from the powers of darkness. In the name of Jesus I pull down every stronghold, I come against every principality and I break every power of the enemy against me, my family and those connected and assigned to me. I decree and declare that we've been delivered from the powers of darkness and translated into the Kingdom of Jesus Christ.

Robed in the righteousness of God through the Lord Jesus Christ, I establish the Kingdom of God over my life, my family and those connected and assigned to me. In the name of Jesus I announce that I have total access to receive every covenant promise as a seed of Abraham, because I've been redeemed from the curse of the law. So I decree and declare that I will not be denied of my benefits; therefore, I enforce every promise and every law that's governed by the Word of God. As I execute and speak God's Word, I employ angels to hearken to the voice of God's Holy Word to bring every spoken Word to pass and in Jesus' name I seal this prayer and decree and declare that it is binding by the Word, the blood and by the Holy Spirit. In Jesus' name, Amen!

WEALTH CONFESSION

I am anointed to prosper, I'm a money magnet and money is drawn to me, in Jesus' name. Money is drawn to me from hidden places and money hunts me down. Goodness and mercy follow after me all the days of my life. Everything that I put my hands to prospers. I'm anointed to make money any and everywhere I go. I'm anointed to draw affluent clients. The affluent are attracted to me; they seek after me because I have what they need.

Prosperity looks good on me and I wear it well. I'm clothed in prosperity. I'm a multimillionaire with multiple streams of income. People hunt me down for my services. I produce millions for the Kingdom of God. I'm a giver and a tither, therefore, the windows of heaven are open to me to pour out a blessing to where there's not enough room to receive. I live under an open heaven and the heavens are opened to me and my household, in Jesus' name.

I live in the overflow of life; therefore, I'm always filled and full. Money is transferred to me now. I receive money today and money comes to me every day. I'm making money while I sleep. Ideas, insight and concepts from the Holy Spirit come to me daily to produce millions. I receive witty ideas that will produce millions in my storehouses. Money is attracted to me everywhere I go. People stop me everywhere I go and ask me what I do, because I wear the garments of wealth. My countenance glows wealth; it shines from me, in Jesus' name.

I only do business with people who can afford my services, unless directed differently by the Holy Spirit. I get paid big for what I do because I'm anointed to do what I do and I'm worth it. People all over this world are seeking after my services. I don't apologize for being blessed and I don't hide my wealth because I'm not ashamed of money and prosperity. I wear the blessing because I am the blessing. God gives me the power to get wealth and I always give Him the glory. No man makes me rich but God.

I control money therefore money never controls me. Money obeys me. My hands are always open to receive and my storehouses and bank accounts are always open to receive, in the name of Jesus. I'll never be broke a day in my life. I always have more than enough and I love to give into the lives of others. I always have to give to others. I give to the poor and I confess that I'm an open channel and portal to which God can give and flow through. My money flows like a river, a steady flow and a steady unending stream. My children are anointed to receive money; they are anointed to prosper always and money comes to them and through them. My children wear the blessing.

God uses me as a true example of who He really is as prosperity and wealth. When people look at me, they see wealth. My name is associated with money, wealth, prosperity, luxury and high-profiles. I have wisdom over my money and I decree and declare that my bank accounts are overflowing continuously forever, in Jesus' name, amen!

LOOSE YOUR MONEY CONFESSION

I declare that I am a money magnet. I command my money to be loosed in the earth daily; therefore, the heavens must loose my money daily.

I decree and declare that money is being loosed right now from the heavens. When I call money, it comes. Money, I call you right now; I command you to come to me right now; I summon you and I decree that you will obey. I talk to money and I say "Money I control you, you will never control me; therefore, money- you must obey me now."

Everywhere I go, the manifestation of money shows up in my life because I attract money; I never chase money. Money hunts me down, it looks for me, it knows how to find me and it finds me daily. Goodness and mercy follow after me all the days of my life. Money follows and chases after me everywhere I go. Every day there is a divine manifestation of money in my bank accounts. My bank accounts are filled with thousands of dollars daily.

I make money every day. I call money to my bank accounts right now.

Money, I command you to manifest yourself. I am anointed to reap; therefore, I reap what I sow and I sow money because I am a seed sower; as I sow, money comes back to me and men give to my life daily; good measure, pressed down, shaken together and running over. The windows of heaven are wide open to me, pouring out a blessing that there will not be room enough to receive, causing an overflow of the blessing in my life. Money overflows in my personal life, business and bank accounts. Money is flowing in me like a river right now; it never stops flowing. I have the ability and power to produce as much money as I desire whenever I get ready because the source of money lives in me. Ideas, insight and concepts from the heavens come to me daily to produce millions. Millionaire status is in my DNA; it abides and dwells in me. I produce millions of dollars daily because I am a money maker. When people come in contact with me, they come in contact with money. I am known all around the world as "The God Made Millionaire" and People call me Kim K. Sanders (replace with your name) the Money Maker. I am fruitful and I multiply like My God, producing continuously after my own kind, therefore, I produce other millionaires. I reproduce my success into my children and into the lives of those that sit before me. I decree and I declare that I will never in my life be broke. I detest poverty and I am allergic to being broke. I decree that anything broke that comes into my presence must be fixed because I am a money maker; I make, construct, build and produce money makers.

I make money come into existence and into my presence with my seeds and my words, because I have been given the power to get wealth.

God is the author of money; He has written the book and He has given me the manuscript and the copyright to publish it publicly in my life.

Money rains on me. Money overwhelms me, it overtakes me. I am saturated with money, from the top of my head to the soles of my feet. I make money while I am sleeping. Money is making its way to me right now. When I talk to money, money listens, "so money you must obey because I have authority over you, therefore I command you to be loosed from the heavens."

I am a money attracter. Money comes to me unhindered. Money flows to me like a river a constant steady flow. Money finds me daily. It comes into my presence. I produce hidden treasures of secret places. There is not a day that goes by that I don't make money. Money comes to me from hidden places. I receive money right now. My countenance says money. When people look at me, they see money. When people come into my presence, they give to me. My countenance demands that people sow into my life. Everywhere I go, I run into money. Money obeys me quickly; as fast as I call it, money comes.

PROSPERITY CONFESSION

I am prosperous. Prosperity is who I am. It belongs to me. It is in my DNA. When people see me, they see prosperity because I am prosperity.

I am prosperous in all that I do. Everything I put my hands to, it prospers because prosperity lives in me. It abides in me. It dwells in me. It overflows in me because I fill myself with prosperity food. I have a prosperous mind, soul and body. I live a prosperous life, because I represent God in the earth. God is prosperity, therefore I am prosperity. Total life prosperity is my portion.

God has given me the power to get wealth; therefore, I have the ability, the endowment and power to have wealth. The prosperity anointing is flowing in my life. Everything I do and touch prospers. I am clothed in prosperity and prosperity looks good on me. Prosperity saturates my mind and soul;

I think prosperous thoughts daily. I am subject to the spirit of prosperity only, therefore, I refuse, reject and resist poverty and I am allergic to being broke.

I have a prosperity vocabulary, which causes me to have a prosperous mouth. I speak prosperity to my spirit, soul and body. I speak prosperity to my business, therefore, my clients and customers are prospering. I speak prosperity to my bank accounts; therefore, I decree and declare that there will be a divine manifestation of money in my bank accounts today because prosperity belongs to me. It is a part of my covenant.

I say that I have prosperous relationships, starting with my family. My family is prosperous. My children are prosperous and prosperity lives and abides in my home. Prosperity rests in my atmosphere. Everywhere I go, I prosper. I deposit prosperity into the lives of others. I am a prosperity guru.

I produce prosperity. When people look at me, they see prosperity.

Prosperity recognizes me everywhere I go. Prosperity is subject to me. My name (put your name in it) is associated with prosperity. I represent prosperity, riches and wealth in the earth. When people hear my name, they think prosperity. When people see me, they say, (say your name here) is prosperous. I draw prosperity to me, I attract prosperity to me and I associate with prosperity only. I was born to be prosperous and my whole life represents total life prosperity in the earth, in the name of Jesus.

I'M STRONG

Father, I thank you that I'm not moved by negative circumstances around me. I'm not moved by adversity and calamity around me or the drama of others, but I'm only moved by the Word of God. I decree and declare that I am strong mentally, emotionally and physically. I'm unstoppable, prospering in all that I put my hands to. I'm unmovable, always abounding in the Word and in the work of the Lord. I'm anchored in the Word of God. My roots are deeply planted. The Word is deep in the hard drive of my heart, my spirit and my soul, therefore absolutely nothing or no one can uproot me.

I'm not moved by what's going on in the world's system. I will not submit to the blueprints or mindset of the world's system. I will not be seduced by religion in the world's system or the world's way of doing things. I will not be held captive or in bondage by the world's system. I will rule and reign in the midst of the world's recession, by recession-proofing my home with the security of being subject to the spirit of life in Christ Jesus ONLY.

I decree and declare that I am pregnant with life. I speak life to everything around me. I speak life in my home, to my husband, to my children, to my family, to my body, to my finances, to my ministry, to my business and to every situation that looks me in the face, in the name of Jesus. I trust in the Lord with my whole heart and I don't lean to my own understanding, but I acknowledge Him in all my ways as He directs my path.

I have a solid, firm, permanent, concrete foundation and my stakes are anchored in the kingdom of God's system, as I guard and build my future. Absolutely nothing or no one can shake or break me. No storm, no tornado, no hurricane, no earthquake or blizzard can blow me away because I stand firm with my feet planted, strong and shod with the preparation of the gospel of peace. I wear the whole armor of God at all times. I guard my heart with all diligence and I build my future by speaking the Word of God out of my mouth daily. I meditate God's Word day and night so I may observe to do all that's written and cause good success to come to my household. I live on the offense and not on the defense; therefore, I'm not taken off guard by anything that comes my way because I'm a watchman on the wall. I am not ignorant of satan's devices. I see every strategy, every tactic, every plot and every plan of the enemy. I recognize him in every form and in every disguise, in the name of Jesus. I decree and declare that I'm anointed to loose the bands of wickedness, undo the heavy burdens, let the oppressed go free and break every yoke. The anointing on me is like oil; not only do I become fragrant, but I am able to slip past the enemy. The anointing is equated to fatness, therefore, I decree and declare that I grow fat in God's presence and authority in the name of Jesus.

I decree and declare that my days of discipline and preparation will be compensated with favor. God is favoring me now. Supernatural doors are always opened to me because I have extravagant favor, uncommon favor, unlimited favor and featured status with God and with man everywhere I go. Favor goes before me and encircles me; I release favor right now and I decree and declare that I will not be denied, in the name of Jesus.

THE BLESSING

Father, in the name of Jesus, as a Prophet of God, I pronounce the blessing over the person reading these words and I decree and declare that the blessing rests upon their life.

Dear reader, I pronounce and release the Prophet's anointing upon your life in the name of Jesus. I release divine prosperity, divine protection, divine wisdom, divine manifestations, divine guidance, divine intervention, divine insight, divine enabling, divine favor and divine health.

I release you into the third realm and declare that your name is associated with riches, wealth, luxury, greatness, integrity, goodness, extravagance, preeminence, prominence, preferential treatment and featured status. I decree and declare that you are overtaken with blessings. I say that you are blessed in the city, blessed in the field, blessed when you come, blessed when you go, I decree that you are blessed to achieve fruitfulness in every area of your life. I call you blessed; spirit, soul and body.

I declare that the Lord blesses the works of your hands and provides work opportunities, advancement, profits and bonuses. I say that everything you put your hands to prospers. I declare strategic positioning, unexpected gifts, favorable settlements, wealth transfers, secret riches and hidden treasures in your life.

I declare that you have favor with creditors, until your bills are paid in full and I prophesy that you are debt free. I declare that you have multimillion dollar ideas, strategies of increase and multiplication that produces multiple streams of income. I seal this blessing by the name and the blood of Jesus and I bless you NOW in Jesus' mighty Name, Amen! RECEIVE IT!

ABOUT THE AUTHOR

As an authorized spokesman for God, Prophetess Kim K. Sanders speaks the prophetic utterances and heart of God. Boldly proclaiming God's message, she speaks of current issues, bringing warning, instructions and reproof, giving insight and foresight, revealing the plans and will of God. Prophetess Kim is a Licensed Ordained Minister, an Anointed Minstrel, Psalmist, Prophetic Spoken Word Poet and Published Author. Prophetess Kim is the Founder and President of Kim K. Sanders Ministries, Inc.

The Arkansas native has an extensive school of the arts background, which includes music, dance and drama. Kim's study of dance began at the age of nine with the late Dot Callanen, where she studied ballet, tap and jazz. She became a company member and performed in several productions. Thereafter, Kim furthered her ballet studies with Antonio Mesa from France and the late Manolo Agullo, at the Arkansas Arts Center. She traveled and appeared in various productions such as "The Red Shoes," "Peter and the Wolf" and many others. Kim later made her debut as a Professional Ballet Dancer in the Senior Company of Ballet Arkansas under the direction of the late Lorraine Cranford. She performed in "The Nutcracker Suite," "Swan Lake" and "Giselle." She also made several solo guest appearances.

Kim's study of Music began at an early age and continued as a Music Major at Cameron University in Lawton Oklahoma. All her life she had a burning passion and deep desire to sing, dance, act and play music; little did she know that God was preparing her all along as a vessel to carry His glory. Kim's gifts are used to set the atmosphere for the Holy Spirit and to accompany her for the preaching of the Word. As Prophetess Kim sings and plays prophetic sounds from heaven, the Mantle of David rests on her to cast out demons. People are brought into the very presence of God, receiving peace, joy and all manner of healings and deliverances as the power of music penetrates the atmosphere and pierces the forces of darkness with the fire of God!

Prophetess Kim has a unique deliverance ministry in which she ministers life to those who are spiritually dead, healing to the brokenhearted and deliverance to those held captive living in bondage to the god of this world. God has given Kim a spirit led boldness to minister truth with confidence, love and the authority that will penetrate directly to the spirit of man, challenging men and women to repentance, obedience and a life of complete wholeness. As a "Spiritual Bulldozer" in the Kingdom of God, Prophetess Kim is continuously disrupting, penetrating and tearing down the powers of darkness; digging deep, uprooting everything that's not of God. Kim is the proud wife of former Circuit Judge Ernest Sanders Jr. and the devoted mother of two children, Trinity Latrice Eubanks and Ernest Sanders III.

Kim is the author of ***"Hushhhh God Is Talking" and "Loose Your Money."*** For more information about online classes, live events and booking Kim, visit www.kimksanders.com.

www.ingramcontent.com/pod-product-compliance
Lightning Source LLC
Chambersburg PA
CBHW070549300426
44113CB00011B/1844